Investing:
Stocks, Options, Gold & Silver, Your Path To Wealth In A Bull Or Bear Stock Market

Free Bonus!!!

We would like to offer you our FREE Guide to jump start you on a path to improve your life & Exclusive access to our Breakthrough Book Club!!! It's a place where we offer a NEW FREE E-book every week! Also our members are actively discussing, reviewing, and sharing their thoughts on the Book of The Week and on topics to help each other Breakthrough Life's Obstacles! With a Chance to win a $25 Gift Card EVERY Month! Please Enjoy Your FREE Guide & Access to the **Breakthrough Book Club** -

https://publishfs.leadpages.co/the-breakthrough-book-club-

Introduction

Do you want to increase your wealth potential? Are you looking to invest your money in productive avenues? If so, then you have reached the right place!

Stock market investments are some of the most lucrative investments in the world. Not only will they help you increase your money's worth, exponentially, but also help you secure your financial future.

In this book, we will look at the different elements of stock market in detail and also its several components. We will understand what each of them is capable of doing for you and your finances.

As a beginner, there are several tricks of the trade that you must know in order to have a good start in the business and avoid certain pitfalls. We will look at these tips and tricks and fully prepare you for the stock market.

Let us start!

Chapter 1: Understanding The Stock Market

In this first chapter of the book, let us read on the basics of the stock market and understand its different elements.

What is the Stock market?

The stock market is a market place where financial instruments are bought and sold on a day-to-day basis. It is a physical market where people converge to trade in these instruments. If you wish to buy and sell stocks and other such financial securities, then you must participate in your local stock market's activities. These stock markets can be physical or virtual in nature. There are several stock markets located all over the world and they are all inter-dependent. Depending on the country to which you belong, you must participate in your local stock market's trade and can also trade in foreign markets if you have the permission to do so.

What is the Share market?

The share market is a part of the stock market. More often than not, people use these terms interchangeably and assume that the stock market and the share market are the same thing. But it is safe to say that the stock market contains the share market along with other types of markets. The share market is where shares are bought and sold on a daily basis. You can trade in these shares by participating in the share market's daily activities. The most popular physical market in the world is the New York Stock Exchange or NYSE and the best virtual market is the NASDAQ. The former has many companies' shares listed from all over the world and the latter has lesser companies listed. You can choose either to trade in.

What are the Brokerage firms?

Brokerage firms are companies that are members of the stock market. In order to trade in the market, you have to be a member in it, first. There are many brokerage firms, which are members of these stock markets. They will help you to trade in the markets. You must look up the best brokerage firms in your area and narrow down to the one that provides the best service. You must also look at the brokerage terms, as all these firms will charge you a certain fee as the brokerage fees. It will differ from firm to firm and you must look at the one that is charging the most reasonable fee. Even if you trade independently you will have to pay the company a fee.

Who are Brokers?

Brokers are employed at these brokerage firms. They will assist you in buying and selling the stocks and other financial securities. Depending on the size of the firm, there can be just a few or several brokers. You can request to be assigned the best broker in the firm to assist you. These brokers are of two types discounted brokers and full time brokers. Discounted brokers are those that will only help you buy and sell your stocks and not assist you in any other way. Full time brokers on the other hand will help you pick the stocks and work for you. The latter will cost you more as compared to the former.

What is a Demat account?

A demat account is one which you will use to carry out your trades. Both you and your broker will have access to it. You will have to add in a certain sum of money to it, which will be used to fund your stock market investments. The broker will call you to confirm that a certain amount is being withdrawn and go ahead only after your approval.

Who should invest?

There is no rule that only certain type of people can invest and anybody interested in increasing their financial capacity can invest in the stock market. If you are wise enough to make the best choices for yourself then you can invest in the stock market and increase your money's potential. Right from a student to a housewife to a businessman, anybody can enter the stock market and invest any amount of their choice.

How long to invest?

That depends on your choice. There are different investment times to choose from. From short term to midterm to long term, you can pick the time that suits you the best. If you are looking for quick results then you can invest short term, if you are looking for long term results then you can invest in long term investments. That choice is for you to make. But before you decide, you must understand each type's pros and cons and only then make your investment. Try to conduct a thorough research before making your investment.

Are results guaranteed?

Nothing is guaranteed in the stock market. If you are looking for guarantees, then you must not invest in the share market. Everything depends on how the market operates and whether it is a good market or a bad one. You have to understand the risks that are involved and what you might lose when you enter the stock market. Then you must look at the profit aspect of it. But despite having no real guarantees, the stock market is one of the most lucrative investment options that you will find and investing in it will help you increase your money's worth through several folds.

What are the gains?

The gains will depend on the type of investment that you make. If you are interested in intraday trade or short-term investments, then you will receive a profit from it. But if you are invested in it for the long term then you will receive a dividend from it. It is possible from you to receive both of these from the same stock. You must choose the type of investment first before choosing the type of capital gain that you wish to receive.

What are safe options?

There are no safe and unsafe options in the stock market. Everything has equal risk attached to it. You must look at the one that helps you attain the maximum benefit and minimize the risk as much as possible. Once you read on all the different forms of stock investments, you can make your choice. There are just a couple of safe options though like government bonds, which we will read about in detail in a future chapter.

Can I invest in all of them?

Yes. It is possible for you to invest in all of them. In fact, it is recommended that you do so as it will help you diversify and spread the risk. You will have the chance to split your profits and losses and not have it come from the same place. A diverse portfolio will allow you to incur maximum benefit and that should be your sole aim when you wish to invest in the stock market.

Is it taxed?

Yes. Any capital gain that you derive from your stock market investments is taxed. Whether you derive a profit or a dividend, you will be taxed for it. The percentage differs from state to state. You have to check with the laws in your state to know how much will be taxed. You have to calculate both the brokerage amount as well as the tax payable before knowing how much you will gain from your stock market transactions.

These form some of the common questions that get asked on the subject and hope you had yours answered.

Chapter 2: What Are Stocks?

In the previous chapter, we looked at some of the basic questions on the stock market and now, let us look at what shares mean.

Meaning

A share, or a stock, refers to a stake in the company's ownership. If you are to buy shares of a company, then you are buying the rights of ownership in that company. This entitles you the right to its profits and losses and also its assets and liabilities. So you have to be willing to partake in both their profits and losses if you wish to hold their shares in your possession.

These shares are all listed in the stock exchange. You must choose a company that you think is a good company to invest in and buy their shares. Your broker will assist you in doing so.

Most traders will look for a share in the different sectors of the stock market. These sectors are divided based on the type of industry that the companies belong to for example; Apple and Microsoft belong to the IT industry. Similarly, there will be the chemical industry, biotechnology, consumer goods etc. Your aim should be to choose a couple of the best industries from each sector and buy their shares.

You must maintain as diverse a portfolio as possible and have several shares that belong to different companies in order to minimize your risk.

You can hold these shares for a short time or long term depending on what you wish to achieve from it. If you are looking for a short-term gain, then you must invest in companies whose share prices differ from day to day. If you are looking for long-term gains, then look for companies that pay you good dividends. If you want both then buy shares of a good dividend paying company just before they announce results and then sell them after results are announced.

How it works

The share market works on the basis of demand and supply. As you know, there are millions of shares in the share market. If a large number of people are favoring a company's shares and are buying it in bulk then the number of shares in the market will reduce, as the demand for it will shoot up. This will automatically cause the company's share price to shoot u as well.

The opposite will happen when the demand for a share will be low. There will be more supply of these shares in the market and less demand. That will cause its price to lower considerably.

This keeps happening throughout the day and it is difficult to say when the prices will rise or fall. If people, see that the price of a stock is rising then they will quickly buy it and do vice versa when the stock's price falls.

It is tough to determine which company's shares will remain in demand and which ones will plummet as it is impossible to understand the mood of the market. However, if you observe the market trends for a few days, you will be able to set a pattern and understand how it works.

Types

There are two main types of stocks that you can choose from and they are known as common stocks and preferred stocks.

Common stocks

Also known as equity stocks, these are stocks that are bought and sold in the share market. The share market is known as the secondary market as people belonging to the companies previously hold these stocks. These stocks are said to be good choices, as it will allow the holders the right to elect the board of members for the company. These stocks are easy to sell, as there will be a big demand for them in the market. However, holders of these stocks will be considered last when it comes to payouts in case the company is winding up.

Preferred stocks

The other type of stocks is known as preferred stocks. Preferred stocks are those that are issued by the company to the top board members and might also offer to the employees. So you either have to be a member of the board of the company or the employee to receive these. These stocks will not allow you the right to elect the board members but you will receive a fixed interest on your investment on a quarterly basis regardless of whether the company is doing good or bad. And these shareholders will be considered first when it comes to paying out at the time of winding up of the company.

Advantages

There are several advantages to investing in the share market. The first advantage is that the shares are extremely liquid and you can buy and sell them with ease. You will have a lot of sellers for a stock you wish to buy and an equal number of buyers to the stocks you wish to sell. Another advantage is the choice that these stocks give you. You can choose to invest in them for a short period or for a long period depending on your needs. The return on your investment will be quite big when you invest in the share market. In fact, it will be bigger than what you would receive from your bank on your savings. So this makes for a great choice for all those looking to increase their money's worth.

Disadvantages

There are certain disadvantages attached to stock investments. The first one being extreme volatility present in the market! The share prices will fluctuate tremendously and you will have to take quick action if you wish to make a profit. The demand and supply chain in the stock market is impossible to predict and you will have a tough time knowing which share is good to buy and which one should be sold. The risk involved in the share market is immensely high. There is a 50 – 50 chance of you making a profit or a loss. There are no guarantees and you must choose the investment that will minimize your risk to a large extent.

These form the various advantages and disadvantages of investing in the share market and you must invest in it after carefully evaluating them.

Chapter 3: What Are Options?

In the previous chapter, we looked at shares in detail and in this one, we will shift focus to options.

Meaning

Options refer to financial instruments that are traded in the stock market. These instruments can be shares, bonds etc. Options are traded on a daily basis and you can choose to invest in these as opposed to shares. Options are a contemporary form of investment options that you can choose and are quite different from regular shares. You will still need to go through your broker if you wish to invest in options and can also employ them to choose the best ones for you.

How it works

The options work in a fairly simple manner. Let us look at an example to understand it better. Suppose someone offers you an old antique telephone. They price it at $500. You are an antique collector and wish to buy it. But you will pay $100 in advance for it and promise to pay the rest in 2 weeks' time. Now, during this time, one of the two following situations might occur

1) During the 2 weeks, you will find out that the telephone belonged to Edison and its actual value is $1000. You will jump at this opportunity and pay the remainder to possess the telephone.

2) The telephone is a fake and is not an antique piece and its actual value is $75. Now, you have the choice to not pay the remainder and can cancel the deal. But you should be willing to forgo the $100 that you paid as advance for it.

This "option" that you have to go through with the deal or reject it is the same option that you will have towards the financial security being traded.

Let us see an example.

X wishes to sell you 50 shares of company ABC priced at $100 each. You will have to pay $5000 towards it. But you will pay $500 as advance and promise to pay the rest in a week's time.

In the week that follows, the company announces its results and the share price rises to $110 each owing to god progress. Now the seller has to give you the shares for the agreed price and cannot demand the changed price. You will benefit from the deal to the extent of $10 per share.

But in a week, the company announces and results and the per share value drops to $90. Now instead of taking a loss of $10 per share, you can refuse to pay for it and allow the payment date to pass by. The trader will keep your $500 and cancel the deal.

This is a good choice to make, as you will end up saving $54500 on the deal.

The right to purchase the option is known as call option and the right to sell the option is known as a put option.

Types

There are two types of options namely European options and American options

European options

European options are those that will not allow you to settle the deal before the maturity period. So say you bought 100 shares on 1 May 2015, which have a maturity period of 1 year. So you cannot sell your shares until 1st May 2016. Even if you have the chance to settle the deal in December 2015 and earn a substantial profit from it, you will have to wait an entire year to settle it. These options are not favored owing to their rigidity.

American options

American options are the most preferred types of options. Here, there is no compulsion for you to hold on to these options until their maturity period. If you wish to dispose it off earlier then you can do so. Say you bought the options on 1 May 2015 and it matures on 1st May 2016, you can settle it in a month's time if it turns out to be a lucrative option for you.

Note: These are mere names and they are not relevant to Europe or America.

Advantages

There are many advantages to choosing options. The first advantage is that, you will have the chance to hedge. Hedging refers to safe guarding your investment. Instead of going all in with your money, you are safe guarding a majority by holding it in your possession. This will reduce your risk of loss by a large margin. Another advantage is that, you can capitalize on your investment at any time and not have to wait on it. This is relevant to the American options and you can use it to your advantage.

Disadvantages

Just as the advantages, there are also certain disadvantages associated with options. The first disadvantage is that, the value of the share might go either way. So you must be prepared to take a loss on the investment and cannot expect to only make a profit on it. Another disadvantage might stem up if the terms of the option are not clearly stated. Discrepancies might arise at the time of settling, which is not desirable for both parties. Sometimes, it is difficult to find good option deals. You have to do some research and find the best ones.

These form the different advantages and disadvantages of options and you must understand these thoroughly before investing in them.

Chapter 4: What Are Precious Metals?

In the previous chapter, we looked at options in detail and in this one; we will focus on precious metals as an investment.

Meaning

The stock market is a vast place where several things are bought and sold on a daily basis. You have to familiarize yourself with each of these in order to choose the best ones.

Just like stocks, precious metals are also traded in the stock market. These precious metals are listed in the bullion market. The bullion market operates independently and you can buy and sell precious metals here.

As you know, precious metals are extremely valuable. When you wish to buy these, you have to understand their true value. You must understand the different factors that affect its prices and know the best price to pay for each type of metal.

Precious metals are sold in grams or kilograms and you must know their prices before buying them. You must also know its purity while buying. It is important to understand that these precious metals will be delivered to you and you will actually be taking possession.

How it works

Precious metal prices are governed by the same rules that govern stocks. They are based on demand and supply principles. If there is a lot of demand for a metal, then its price will be high and if there is less demand then its price will be low.

There are many factors that contribute towards these demand and supply chains and they are explained as under

Political influence

The country's politics will greatly influence the price of gold. The government will have a control over how much gold is being traded in the markets. It will exercise its right to control the amount of gold that is going in and out of the market. There will be a set gold reserve, which will determine the actual amount of gold that can be traded and will also put a limit on how much a single person can trade in a day.

Cultural influence

Gold is also influenced by the cultures of different countries. Some countries associate gold with festivities and people will flock to buy it. This will cause an increase in the demand for gold and increase its value. But after the festivities have subsided, the gold will be sold and its value will drop. Similarly, other cultural influences will affect the price of precious metals and you will see a rise and fall in their values within a short period of time.

Economic influence

The economic structure of a country has a large bearing on a country's bullion market. Economic relations between the different countries of the world and also a country's worth will determine how much gold can be bought and sold. You have to read the news regularly to understand the limitation on the trade.

Special occasions

Special occasions, such as the Olympics and other sports events will cause the price of precious metals to rise. Medals are made out of these metals so its price is bound to rise.

Hoarders

There will be a lot of hoarders in the world, who will hoard on precious metal. This will cause the price to rise considerably. They will then pump it back into the market and cause the price to fall. So you have to know when it is best to buy and sell precious metal.

These are just some of the reasons that can influence the prices of precious metals and there can be other such factors as well. So these prices are extremely volatile.

Types

Gold

Gold is one of the most preferred precious metals in the world. Right from the jewelry industry to other such industries, gold is always in demand. The price of gold is extremely volatile and you must observe it on a day-to-day basis. You must be aware of the different factors that affect it and judge for yourself a rise or fall in the price. You can also buy gold jewelry and use it and then sell it when you wish to make a profit from it. You can also buy and stock on gold bars and biscuits.

Silver

Silver is just as precious as gold. But its value is slightly lower. It is also used in several industries including heavy machinery and dentistry. The price of silver fluctuates more than gold as it is used in many industries. You must buy silver when it is priced low and then sell it when its price rises. You will be left with a profit from it. You can also buy silver jewelry or sterling silverware, which will fetch you, a good price. Silver bars and biscuits will be available in the bullion market.

Platinum

Platinum is the priciest of all precious metals. It is traded in the bullion market just as the other precious metals. Platinum is used in several industries. Its price keeps fluctuating day in and day out. You can buy platinum jewelry and use it. That will also count as an investment.

These are the most popular precious metals and you can choose any of these or all of them to invest in.

Advantages

There are many advantages of choosing precious metals. The first advantage is that, you will have the chance to take full possession of your investment. Another advantage is that, the value of precious metals is universal. What you buy in your country, you can exchange for a good price in another. Another important advantage is that, their value will not be affected during inflation. You can exchange your gold for money and use it to your advantage. You have the chance to further diversify your investment by investing in precious metals. Precious metals are extremely liquid and you can sell it at any point in time. If you are in need of money, then you can quickly sell your gold.

Disadvantages

The major disadvantage of this type of investment is the high price of precious metals. You will be able to buy only a small amount with your investment. Another disadvantage is getting attached to it. Once you hold a form of precious metal with you, you will find it increasingly difficult to let go of it. So you will start hoarding it. In times of economic and political crisis, you will not be able to sell your gold or avail a good price for it. It will be under strict control and you will not be able to profit from it.

These form the different advantages and disadvantages of precious metals and you must understand each one in detail before investing.

Chapter 5: What Are Commodities?

The stock market is vast and apart from shares and precious metals, it also allows people to trade in different commodities.

Meaning

Commodities trading are a form of trading where everyday commodities are traded on a daily basis. These commodities are traded in the stock market and you must be well versed with the different commodities that are traded.

The market for commodities is known as a speculative market where you speculate on the price of the commodities. The difference in your buy and sell price will make for your profit or loss. Many people prefer to start with commodities trading as it will give them a fair idea of how the markets work. The payoff from it is also quite substantial making it a great choice for beginners.

How it works

Each commodity has a specific value attached to it. The commodity is worth a price, based on the value that it provides the end user. It is governed by the principle of demand and supply. You have to bid for these commodities and once they are allotted to you, you must speculate on their future prices. There will be a time frame within which you must speculate and dispose of your stock.

These commodity prices are affected by several conditions such as the following:

Weather

Weather is the primary factory that affects commodities. As you know, the weather can influence crops, livestock etc. If there is a lot of snow, then crops such as potatoes and oranges will be affected negatively. This will directly affect their pricing. Similarly, too much or too little rain, erratic sunlight and other such weather conditions will have a direct bearing on the commodities. You must read the newspaper on a daily basis to understand these and also subscribe to websites that will supply you with important news articles based on your commodities trading.

Political scenario

The political scenario in a country will have a large bearing on the commodities. Gold, silver and other metals' trade will be governed by the political wing of a country and you must be well versed with your country's policies. Be on the lookout for news articles that tell you about political upheavals, which will be clear indicators for you to tread carefully in the commodities market.

Economic conditions

There are certain economic conditions that can affect the prices of commodities. In case of inflation, the prices will surge up and when deflation occurs, the prices will drop. You have to invest as per the economic situation and do whatever is right in the current scenario.

Cultural influence

Just like how precious metals are influenced by cultural differences, commodities are also affected in the same manner. If a festival comes by, then people will buy lots of produce, which will increase its prices, as soon as the festival passes by, the prices will fall again owing to reduced demand.

Other

Other factors such as war or political disputes amongst countries, farmer strikes etc. also influence the prices of commodities. The commodities market is highly volatile and the prices can change drastically in a matter of seconds.

Types

There are different types of commodities that are traded in the market. Let us look at each of them in detail

Agricultural produce

Agricultural produce such as vegetables, fruits, sugar, corn, oats, wheat, rice etc. are all traded in the commodities market. These are listed in large quantities and you must bet on their final price based on the different conditions that are prevalent in the market.

Chemicals

Industrial chemicals and solvents are also traded in the market. These chemicals are required by industries on a daily basis to prepare soaps, detergents, cosmetics etc. So their prices vary all through the day. You must bid for these and speculate on their future price.

Livestock

Livestock is also traded on a daily basis. Livestock such as goat and chicken as well as meats such as pork and lamb are traded. These are heavily used in the food industry and their prices fluctuate all through the day. You must buy these early in the morning and dispose them off by nightfall in order to avoid the risk of price changes.

Metals

Metals such as nickel, lead and iron are used in industrial processes and products. These industries will always require these metals and their prices will keep varying all through the day.

Energy

Energy resources such as gas and oil are also listed in the commodities market. As you know, these are heavily used in the automotive, cosmetic, clothing and chemicals industries. You can bet on their prices as well and earn a profit.

These form the different categories of commodities traded in the market and it is best that you invest in all of these to diversify your portfolio.

Advantages

There are several advantages of investing in commodities. The main advantage is that, you can diversify your portfolio by investing in commodities. Another advantage is the high rate of return that you can receive on your investment. But the main advantage is the chance to indulge in hedging. Hedging refers to safeguarding your investment in case of inflation.

Disadvantages

The main disadvantage of investing in commodities is that, money management will turn tricky. It will also be important for you to anticipate losses, as these investments will not always turn out well for you.

Chapter 6: What Is Foreign Currency?

Meaning

As you know, differs countries make use of different currencies and there is no such universal money that is accepted in the world. In the U.S. we make use of dollars and in Europe, the euro is used to make purchases. Now suppose you wish to buy wine from Italy. You can't pay the Italian trader in dollar and must pay up him in euro. So, for that to happen, you will exchange your dollars for euros and buy the wine.

This exchange is better known as foreign exchange. Foreign exchange, or better known as forex, deals with exchanging the currency of one country with that of another. This exchange does not happen in the stock market like how regular stocks are traded. Two people from different countries will enter into a deal with another to exchange their individual currencies. This type of deal is compared to a proverbial   handshake.

So if you wish to exchange your dollars with Japanese yen, then you must contact a dealer of yen to help you convert your currency.

How it works

These currencies that belong to different countries of the world will all differ in their values. So $1 will not be equal to €1 or ¥1, it will differ in value based on the country's economic standing. When these currencies are pitted against one another, one will always trail and the others value will be greater. The person, whose currency value is greater, will benefit from the deal, as he will receive more of the foreign currency. Say for example a $1 bill is worth ¥10. If a person exchanges $10 then he will receive ¥100. This is a good thing, as he will get more money to his credit. His next move will be to exchange the yen for another country's currency that is even lower and then convert back all of it into dollars to realize a profit.

Another way to trade is to buy foreign currency and hold on to it until such time as its value rises. This will ensure that the person rings in a profit.

Types

There are many currencies in the world including the American dollar, the European euro, the Japanese yen, the Chinese Yuan, the Indian rupee etc. Each ones price is regulated by their respective country's trade policies and government   norms.

You must check with your local Fred tracing bank for the current prices and not merely do a Google search. Once you know the price of the currency calculate the exchange rate with your local currency and decide whether or not you wish to carry out the trade. These currency prices are quite volatile and   will   change   from   day   to   day.

Advantages

The main advantage of carrying out foreign trade is that, it gives the investor a lot of leverage. Just a small investment can fetch great profits in no time. But it is important to understand which currency will pay the best price. Another important advantage of forex trading is that, the trading hours are flexible as the market is open 24 hours. This is unlike the stock market that opens in the morning and closes by evening. You can time your working hours based on the country's timings with which you wish to trade.

Disadvantages

The main disadvantage of forex is that, it is easy for you to lose your money given the extreme volatility. Another disadvantage is that, you have to have super-fast Internet connection and an international call facility that will allow you to make calls fast enough. Even if you get late by a couple of seconds then you will miss out on an opportunity to make good money. Another important thing to be wary of are scammers who disguise themselves as foreign exchange traders but will scam you.

Chapter 7: What Are ETFs?

Meaning

Etfs stand for exchange transfer funds. Etfs are traded in the stock market like regular stocks. These etfs are priced at a certain value, which is their value in the stock market. You have to buy them at the bid price and sell at the ask price.

How it works

These etfs are compared to mutual funds. They are mini mutual funds that have several financial securities condensed in them. These etfs are listed in the stock market and you can choose any one depending on their bid price. You must then wait on its price to rise before selling it for a profit.

Types

Fixed income funds

Fixed income funds refer to those that will help you receive a fixed income on a monthly basis. The rate of interest will depend on your investment volume.

Currency funds

Currency funds are those that are invested in foreign markets. So they make use of foreign currencies. This is a great choice for all those looking to diversify their portfolio and invest in foreign markets.

Real estate funds

Real estate funds are better known as REITs. The company that floats these is made to pay 90% of their income to the shareholders. This makes these a lucrative investment opportunity for people to choose.

Commodity funds

Commodity funds are those that invest in different types of commodities and they are split into different units that are distributed to the shareholders.

These form the different forms of etfs that you can choose from. It is best to have one of each to diversify your investments.

Advantages

The main advantage of investing in etfs is the diversification of financial instruments that you can invest in at once. You have the chance to invest a little in precious metals, some in commodities, some in stocks etc. There is no issue with timing your investments and you can choose any viable time to invest in etfs.

Disadvantages

The main disadvantage of etfs is their slow movement. It might take you a lot of time to realize a profit on your investment and so; they are not ideal for intraday investments. It will be tough for you to find dividend yielding etfs; you will have to look keenly to find well-paying etfs.

Chapter 8: What Are Bonds?

Meaning

Bonds are financial securities that are issued by companies to investors with a promise of returning the money within a set period of time along with an added interest. These bonds are issued at a price less than its actual face value to enable the investor to sell it, in case he wishes to dispose it off. Bonds are stock market investments that are preferred by both new comers and old hands owing to their high pay off rate.

How it works

The government or different companies issue bonds in order to raise money for their projects. These companies and governments will promise to pay a rage of interest on the principle sum collected. Say for example Company ABC issues a bond worth $100 to a person and promises to pay 10% interest on it for a year. At the time of maturity, the person will receive $110 on exchange of the bond. These bonds are exchanged based on trust and in hope that the company delivers its promise.

Types

There are five main types of bonds and they are explained as under

Government bond

Government bonds are those that are issued by your national government. This is the most issued type of bond in the world. The national government will issue bonds in order to raise capital for its projects. It will then pay a certain interest on the investment. This interest is generally much higher than what your bank would pay you on your savings account. These are the safest options that you can choose as the government will ensure that you get your money back.

Federal bond

Federal bonds are those that are issued by your local government. The same rules apply to these bonds and are much preferred by investors. The rate of interest paid by these bonds will be higher than what your regular government bonds will pay. These bonds are just as safe as the previous type.

Agency bond

Agency bonds are issued by companies, which are affiliated with the government. So the government will fund these subsidiary companies but not have a control over them. These companies will require capital for the same reasons and collect it from the investors. These bonds do not come with government guarantees and you should be prepared to take a loss if the project does not prove to be fruitful.

Company bond

Company bonds are those that are issued by multinational companies. Say for example Apple wishes to expand their R&D center. They will require a lot of money that no bank will be willing to pay. So, they will reach out to the public for the money by issuing bonds. They will pay an interest and then return the money in full. Here too, you must be prepared to take a loss in case the company's project doesn't do too well. However, most companies deliver on their promise and you might also stand the chance to get their shares at a reduced price.

Zero coupon bond

Zero coupon bonds are those that are issued at a much lower price than their actual value. At the time of maturity, you will receive its full value. If a bond is worth $1000, it will be issued at $500 and carry a maturity period of 2 years. You can exchange the bond in 2 years for $1000. These types of bonds are safe investment options.

Advantages

the main advantage of bonds is the high rate of return on investment. You can invest just a small amount and receive a big profit on it. Another advantage is that, you will receive a systematic monthly interest on your investment. It will be easy for you to avail a bind as it only takes a few minutes for these to be issued. You can shift your bad investments into these safe options.

Disadvantages

The main disadvantage of investing in bonds is credit risk. Another risk is that you will have to wait a long time before realizing a profit. There is also the risk of the project not working out and you losing your investment.

These form the various advantages and disadvantages of bonds but they are overall a better investment choice for you.

Chapter 9: What Are Bullish and Bearish Markets

When we speak of stock markets, we often tend to ignore the very basics. We focus more on the financial instruments that are traded and concentrate less on other aspects such as the condition of the market, timing your investments etc. In this chapter, we will look at 4 types of market conditions, which will help you invest your money at the right time.

Bullish market

A bullish market refers to one, where all the stocks are looking up and are doing well. Bullish market comes from the Bull's style of attacking its prey. The bull is known to bend down and fling its prey into the air using its horns; similarly, the bullish market swoops down and flings all the stocks into the air. The bullish market is known as a seller's market as everybody will be interested in selling their stocks, in order to realize a profit.

You must observe the trend in the market carefully to know whether it is truly in a bullish state or it is only a false alarm. The best way to check is by looking at all the top stocks in each sector. If all of them are in the green, then it is a bullish market. If they are partially in green and partially in red, then it is not a bullish market.

But if the stocks that you are holding are doing well then sell them off at the earliest. It is a general rule of the stock markets that a bullish market will convert into a bearish market without any formal announcements. So it is better to dispose of the stock at the earliest and book your profits instead of waiting on it to go any further.

Bearish market

The bearish market is the opposite of the bullish market. As the name suggests, the bearish market is named after the bear's style of attacking its prey. Just like how the bear swoops down with its paws to attack its prey, the bearish market swoops down and takes with all the stock prices. So all stocks, regardless of company stature and reputation, will remain in red and the market, as a whole will look bad for investors.

However, many contrarians and regular traders see it as a good opportunity for them to buy fresh stock and accumulate on existing stock, as the prices will be low.

The bearish market is not the right time to sell your stocks, as you will have to settle for a loss on your profits. Although it is tough to predict how long the bearish market will last, it is best to wait it out before making a decision on it. If your particular stock is showing no signs of improving even after a year, then it is best to dispose it off and buy a better stock with the same money. Remember that the money you free today will only flow back into your account after 4 days, until such time you must not sit idle as the stock market will not wait for you.

Bullish bar reversal

A bullish bar reversal occurs on a particular stock or a group of stocks belonging to the same sector. It is a situation where, today's lowest price for the stock will be lower than yesterday's and the current price of the stock will be higher than what was yesterday's highest. This is a good situation and it shows that the stock's price is climbing. This generally happens when the traded volumes increase considerably and the number of buyers exceeds the number of sellers.

You can choose to sell off your stocks when this reversal occurs, especially if it is a stock that has been doing badly for some time. If you think it is a good time to exit on the stock, then do so immediately instead on waiting on it to move up any further.

Bearish bar reversal

The bearish bar reversal is the opposite of the bullish bar reversal. In a bearish bar reversal, the stock's days highest will be higher than its previous day's highest price and the current price will be lower than its previous day's low.

This indicates that there has been a massive sell off of the stock and so its prices have dropped. The volumes traded will be low and there will be more sellers and fewer buyers. It is best that you not sell your stock in such a situation. Hold on to it and allow the prices to rise again. But it will be a good time for you to buy the stock or accumulate on it, as the prices will be low.

If you participate in any message board activities on stock market related websites, you can know whether a stock has reversed in a bullish way or a bearish way and act on it accordingly.

These form the different market conditions that you need to familiarize yourself with when you wish to invest in the stock market.

Chapter 10: General Tips On Trading

When you start trading, there are many things that you must do correctly and here are some tips for you to consider before you start investing.

Research

The very first thing you should do is, conduct a thorough research on the subject at hand. This book has provided you with quite a bit of information, no doubt, but you must not stop at that. You must keep your mind enthusiastic and read more on the subject to expand your mind's horizon. Look up information on the Internet and go through other books on trading.

Study daily

You must sit down with a pen and paper and write your daily experience. You will have the opportunity to walk away with new information on a daily basis and it is best that you jot it down in order to remember it better. Keep referring to your notes to understand a particular situation in a better manner. Say for example you witnessed a loss today, jot down what led to it so that you don't repeat the same mistakes again. Similarly, jot down your success story so that you know when to apply the same winning strategy again.

Risk capital

Risk capital refers to money that you are willing to risk losing in the market. As you know, the stock market will put forth both profits and losses. You cannot expect to always remain in profit and must calculate how much you might end up losing after an investment goes bad. Those who venture into investing without calculating their risk capital will find it very difficult to sustain themselves. Have a number or a percentage and work as per it. Ideally, you must have a 5 to 10% loss margin and not any more than that.

Gut instinct

Many times, you will be presented with a situation where you will not be sure of the next move. You will think one thing and your broker will suggest another. If ever such a situation, were to arise, then you must go with your gut instinct. Trust in yourself and go forth with confidence. Those who hesitate and not make quick decisions will end up making a mistake. If you think you will be doing the right thing by selling a bad stock when it dips, then do it without pondering too much over it!

Day trading

Day trading is a great option for you to try out as a beginner. It allows you to buy and sell your stocks in a single day. You have to understand how you can buy these stocks at their lowest prices and then dispose them off at their highest. You will earn a good profit by doing so. Day trading, however, requires due diligence and you must understand its pros and cons before taking it up. The pros include making a good profit within a single day with very little to no investment and the major con includes taking a loss on a bad stock.

Stop loss

When it comes to day trading, you must make use of a stop loss mechanism. Many people prefer to not make use of it out of fear of losing the invested money. But in fact, not making use of a stop loss mechanism will do that. Your broker will suggest an ideal stop loss for your stock and you must either agree with him or choose another number that you think is befitting. Your stop loss mechanism will help you take a small loss, which is perfectly fine given; how you might lose a lot more in the absence of it.

Afternoon trading

It is advisable to trade in the afternoons as opposed to the mornings. The ideal time to trade is between 12 and 2. This is the time when the stocks will dip and rise, in succession. So say a stock reaches its lowest at 12.15, you must then sell it around 1.30, provided it has reached its highest value. If you wish to hold on to the stock then well and good, you can gain from overnight changes in the stock's price. Those looking for long term investing should also pick this time slot to buy their stocks.

Observe the volumes

Whenever you wish to buy the stock of a company; look at its trading volumes to understand its liquidity position. You should see how many people are selling it and how many are buying it. That will give you an idea of its popularity. If there are many buyers and many sellers, then the prices will keep fluctuating. If the buyers are more than the sellers, then the price will remain high. If there are many sellers and little buyers, then the stock's price will fall down considerably. Choose the latter stocks while buying and wait for them to reach the former's position while selling.

Penny stocks

Penny stocks are good choices for you, if you are looking to invest a small sum in the stock market. These stocks are priced at $5 or less. You can buy them in bulk when they hit lowest and sell them at their highest. Penny stocks are mostly traded over the counter so you have to familiarize yourself with that. You must also understand paper trading, as that is what will be predominantly used in penny stock trading.

No greed

Remember to leave all your emotions outside the door when you wish to invest in stock markets. Don't get emotionally attached to a stock or a company. When the right time to sell comes, you won't be able to do so and might have to take a loss on it. Similarly, don't be too greedy. If your stock reaches your target price, then dispose it off at the earliest instead of waiting for it to move up any further. You will end up regretting it later.

These form just some of the tips that you need to bear in mind while you start investing but there are many more such that will make your experience better.

Chapter 11: Getting Started

When it comes to the stock market, there are a few standard steps that you should follow before getting started with it. Let us look at them in this chapter.

Computer

It is obvious that you will need a computer in order to start buying and selling the stocks. You will need a place to set it up and go about your buying and selling. You can choose a quiet corner in your house to set up the system, where you can concentrate on the stocks. It is best to dedicate a whole computer to it instead of using your regular laptop. Once you have your computer set up, you can move to the next step.

Trading account

When you wish to buy and sell stocks, you need to go through a trading firm. These firms will be a member of the stock market and you can buy and sell stocks through their membership. So, you will have to look for the best company to open your trading account with. You can ask friends and family for the best one. The procedure to open an account is fairly simple. All you have to do is provide them with some proof that they will need and they will open the account for you. It might take 24 hours or so for the account to activate. Once done, they will provide you with a login id.

Software setup

The next step is for you to set up the software. The software refers to what you will be using to buy and sell the stocks. The company you are trading with will install it for you or ask you to download it from their website. Although you can login to your account and modify your portfolio, it is always best to have offline access to it as well as it will help you do more. This step generally does not take too much time.

Agent

The next step is for you to find a good agent or broker. You will need brokers and agents to buy and sell the stocks for you. These will have easy access to the stock market and will be able to purchase and dispose of the stocks for you. You can choose between a full time and a part time broker. The former will help perform research on stocks, find the best companies for you to invest with etc. whereas the latter will only buy and sell the stocks and nothing more. The former will charge you quite a bit whereas the latter will charge you nominally for the service they provide.

Research

The next step is for you to do some research on the market. It is not wise for people to buy and sell stocks without doing some due research. You have to look up the companies and check how they are doing. You should also research the precious metals and the other financial securities that you wish to invest with. You can pick a few sectors and find the best companies to invest with. Once you have your top companies. You should observe their trends for a couple of months. You should then pick a few that you think will work well for you and cancel out the others.

Buying

Once you have the stocks, options, precious metals etc. ready, you should place an order to buy them. You should understand that it would take some time for the order to go through and for you to get the securities. If it is an IPO that you are applying for, then you might have to wait for a week or so to know if the stocks have been allotted to you. You can always track the progress by logging into your account. If you are not adept at it as yet, then you can get your broker to buy the securities for you.

Selling

Once you have bought the securities, you should wait on them to grow in value. As you know, these financial securities grow in value over time. You have to wait for them to increase in value before deciding to sell them. Once you think they have reached the ideal price or the target price, you should dispose them off. A good trader will always be proactive and know exactly when to dispose of his securities. You can make use of the trigger system that automatically sells the securities as soon as the ideal price is reached.

Watch list

It is a wise choice for you to prepare a watch list for your stocks. The watch list will contain names of the companies that you have invested in along with details of its price, the number of buyers, number of sellers etc. All of these will help you know the trend that the stock will follow and can make a choice on whether to sell it or hold on to it based on the same.

Writing down

It is important for a new investor to track his or her moves and also record their experiences. They should write down what they experienced in the stock market and how their journey is going. Keeping a record of it will help them refer back to it at any time in the future and also keep them from making some of the mistakes that they might commit during the initial stages.

These form the different things that you need to do in order to get started with the stock market and it is best that you follow this particular sequence.

Chapter 12: Companies to Invest With

It is obvious that you will have to choose some good companies to invest your hard earned money with. You cannot have a random list of companies and you should go about it in a fixed manner. In this chapter, we will look at some aspects of companies that you have to look into before buying their stocks.

You should note that the strategies would differ for day traders and long-term investors.

Reputation

First and foremost, you have to consider the reputation of the company, which might or might not be a fortune 500 company. There can be some companies that deal in illegal goods and even if their stock prices were high, it would be a risk for you to invest with them. So, you have to understand what the company deals with and whether what they make is legal. You should also steer clear of companies that have a lot of internal bickering. The company should have a good foundation and a powerful list of board members, capable of running the company smoothly.

Age

The age of the company also plays a part in the rise and fall in its stock prices. There can be some old companies that are well established with their stock prices remaining pretty stable. On the other hand, there can be some new companies whose prices keep fluctuating owing to bulk buyers and sellers. The case might also be vice versa depending on the market share of the company. You have to pick one based on your appetite for risk. If you wish to invest in a company whose prices fluctuate often then you can pick them but if you want something more stable, then you can pick old and well-established companies.

Sector

The next step is to see how it ranks in the market. As you know, the stock market is divided into different sectors and each sector has a collection of companies. You should pick the sector to which the particular company belongs and check where it stands. Some companies lie right on top while others lie at the bottom. It is always a wise choice to invest with companies that lie on top, or are better known as the sector leaders. These will fare well in the market as compared to those companies that lie at the bottom of the sector.

Reports

It is important for you to look at the charts and graphs of the company and also their reports to know if they are safe investments. Better known as technical and fundamental analysis, you will have to go through the company's official reports to see if they are good to invest with. We will look at both the technical and fundamental analysis that you have to conduct for the stock market as well as the forex market in later chapters of this book.

News updates

It is important to have your eye on news stories in order to find the best companies to invest with. This means that you should subscribe to websites that will keep sending you news alerts about companies and news that will impact the stocks of the company. There can be many stories such as mergers, collaborations, dissolution etc. All of these will have an impact and you should have the latest news about them.

Debts

If a company has a lot of debts, then it will not prove to be a good investment choice. What is the point of investing with a company that is in dire straits owing to a lot of debts? Even if its stock is doing well, it will not continue that way for long. You have to see how much capital they have and how much they owe. You should see whether they would be able to repay the debts within the estimated period. If so, then you can consider the company for medium or long term. If not, then it is best to steer clear.

Profits/ losses

The next step is to look at the profits or losses that the company has been declaring. Don't think it is only the responsibility of the long-term investor to check these. The intraday trader should be equally interested in it, as both these aspects will have an impact on the value of the stocks. You should see the value of the dividend that the company is paying and whether it has been paying the same for some time. Based on what you find, you can invest with the company.

Shareholders

Sometimes, it pays to check the type of crowd that has invested with a particular company. If there are some big shots that are in it for the win, then you too should invest in the company. On the other hand, if there are some day traders that buy and sell on a daily basis thereby affecting the prices of the stocks, then it is better for you to wait until the price of the stock stabilizes or steer clear altogether. However, if you don't have the patience to hold on to a stock like the former, then you can avoid it completely. You can settle for the latter instead, especially if you know how to buy and sell stocks fast.

These are some of the different aspects that you should look into. Remember that it is not limited to just these and there can be many other criteria to consider before making an investment.

Chapter 13: Ideal Stocks to Look For

Just like the best companies to invest with, you should also pick the right stocks. It is important to sometimes separate the company from the stock, as the two might not be related closely. This is especially important for day traders. Here are the aspects to consider for it.

High volume

It is important for you to pick stocks that are being traded in high volumes. As was mentioned before, you can create a watch list for yourself that will contain the different stocks that you have invested in. similarly, you can create a separate watch list that will contain the stocks that you wish to keep an eye on. There, add in the stocks that are being traded in high volumes. The volume will determine the price of the stock. Remember that slow moving stocks will be quite stable and their price will rise or fall very slowly. This can be a bit frustrating for some and they will prefer to pick the ones that are being bought and sold in large volumes. These will move quite fast.

Fluctuations

If a stock price is fluctuating quite a bit, then it might not be an ideal choice for those wanting to have something more reliable in their portfolio. These stocks generally fluctuate owing to day traders that buy and sell them on a minute-to-minute basis. So, it is important to stay away from such stocks. You, can, however, pick them if you wish to invest in something that gives you short bursts of profits. These types are ideal for small investors looking to invest in penny stocks.

Broker's call

The broker sometimes has a very big say in a stock's pricing. There might be a few unions of brokers that will all invest in the same stock and cause its value to rise. So, if your broker has some insider news and is suggesting a particular stock then you can give it a try. It is best to invest a little first and if it looks lucrative then you can invest some more in it. The idea is to invest wisely instead of going all out and investing all at once.

Under-valued

There can be some under-valued stocks that you can invest in. these refer to good stocks that are not being traded in the market on a big scale. Many reasons can contribute towards these stocks being traded in a low manner. Some of them include low volumes, not much information about the company etc. We will look at this aspect in detail in a future chapter of this book.

Message boards

Some websites will have forums and message boards where people discuss stocks in detail. They will have access to some inside information based on which they will suggest some stocks for you to buy. These stocks might prove to be lucrative. However, there might also be some bashers. These refer to people that will purposely bash a stock in order to crush it. If someone is doing so, then it is best to exit from the stock. It might seem like these people will not be able to control the stocks but they will at least cause the prices to fall by quite a bit. If you don't wish to be at the receiving end of it then you better withdraw from the stocks at the earliest.

These form just some of the criteria that you have to consider is not limited to just these. There can be more that you should look into and ensure that you are picking the right ones to invest with.

Chapter 14: Stock Prediction Methods

It is important for you to know where a particular stock is headed. For that, you have to make use of certain techniques that will help you make the predictions.

Before we look at the prediction techniques, we must first look at some trading techniques that you can implement in the stock market.

Trading techniques

Intraday trading

Intraday trading refers to buying and selling stocks and other financial securities within the same day. You don't have to wait a long time to buy or dispose of the stocks. All you have to do is buy them in the morning and then sell them at day's end. It is as simple as that. But for that, you have to have relevant experience and some amount of confidence. You cannot start trading intraday without having enough experience, as you will end up making a mistake. Intraday trading is quite popular with old hands, as they will know when to buy the securities and when to sell them. You can remain with a lot of profit just by knowing which stocks will do well within the day and invest in them at the right time.

Stop loss trading

The next strategy that is important to apply is the stop loss strategy. The stop loss technique is one where the trader pre-decides on where to sell or exit the position. This means that he or she will pick a certain price where the stock can exit at or be sold at. Say for example you buy a certain stock at $5 in the morning. You decide to place a stop loss at $4.95 and a sell call at $8. So, as soon as the price reaches $4.95, it will automatically exit. This is done in a bid to prevent the stock from falling any further and causing you a loss. On the other hand, the stock will help you ring in a profit if you choose the best sell price for it.

Swing trading

The next trading technique is known as swing trading. Swing trading, as the name suggests, refers to a trader who exits his position at the stop loss point. He will then assume a fresh position from the same point. It might sound a bit strange but is a valid technique that both old hands and new traders choose. Now say for example the stock exited at $4.95. The trader will decide to buy more stocks at the same price assuming that it will rise up. It is up to the trader now to place a stop loss price again or avoid it altogether.

Scalping

Scalping is the next technique that traders use. This is a day trading strategy and will mostly suit those that are adept at day trading. Here, the person will buy a stock and then dispose it off within a few minutes or seconds. The trader will not wait on it and will dispose it off as soon as the price rises. Now say you bought a stock at $5 at 10.30 am. The price rises to $5.96 at 10.34 am. You will immediately sell it to attain a profit. This technique is great no doubt but not ideal for beginners. It is better to have some relevant experience first and then indulge in it.

Prediction methods

Here are some prediction techniques that you can pick to predict stock price changes.

Rebate trading

Rebate trading refers to buying and selling stocks through ECN's. These stand for electronic communication networks that help in hosting investments. These ECN's will in turn earn a commission for bringing in the investors and so; a correlated financial system will be put into place. Rebate trading is great for people who are just starting out in the stock market, as it will provide them with the best platform to invest their money. They will not have to do too much research and only invest their money. However, it is important to pick the right ECN to invest with.

Range trading

Range trading refers to sticking to a particular range when it comes to buying and selling stocks. This means that the person will choose the high and the low prices and choose to remain within it. Say for example a person sets the upper limit as $100 and the lower limit as $20. If a particular stock reaches $100 then they will immediately sell it. If it falls below $20 they will do the same. Having a range like this will help in buying and selling the stocks at the right prices.

Candlesticks

Candlesticks trading refer to making using of statistical analysis to predict the trend of the stocks. These candlesticks are placed on a graph where the different prices of the stock are plotted. So right from the highest price to the lowest and also the middle price, the graph will contain all the different price points. Now, it is up to you to calculate the prices that the stock will attain in the near future. This is a great method to use to find the ideal price points and invest in the stock. But since you will have to do quite a bit of calculation, you might need some help with it.

Fibonacci trading

The next statistical tool to employ is known as the Fibonacci method. If you are aware of the Fibonacci number sequence, then you will find it easy to calculate the trends based on it. Just like the series, the prices of the stock will also follow a set pattern. This will make it rather convenient for you to know where the prices are headed. The Fibonacci technique will call for a fair amount of calculations to be made and you have to pull out your calculator for it. However, there are software available that will help you with it. All you have to do is punch in the numbers and the software will give you the result.

Contrarian trading

The next investment method is known as contrarian trading. It is believed that stock market expert Warren Buffet makes use of this technique. As per the contrarian way of investing, the person buys and sells those stocks that are not trending. This means that he or she will buy the stocks that are falling in price and sell the ones that are rising. The contrarian will assume that the stocks that are falling will be good to buy and hold and the ones that are rising will be good to sell and profit from. This technique is said to be quite rewarding but you will have to first identify the best stocks for it.

Trend following

This is the opposite of the previous technique. Here, you will follow the trend of the market instead of going against it. So, if everybody is selling the stock then you too will do the same. And if everybody is buying the stock then you too will buy it. This refers to trend following and is one of the safer techniques to employ. You will not have to take too many risks and will surely gain profits from your transactions.

Price trends

The next prediction method is known as price trends. Price trends are where you look at the trend of the stock and then decide on whether to buy or sell it. Now say a stock is now falling, the investor will assume that the price will rise. He will quickly buy it in anticipation. On the other hand, if the price is rising and reaches a high point, he will assume that the price will begin to fall and dispose of the stock. This type of prediction technique will help you decide on the best stocks to invest with. You will not have to read into it too much and the ideal choices will present themselves with just a little research.

News forecasts

There are some investors that prefer to find their ideal stocks based on what they read in the news. They might find some interesting stocks just by knowing the market's sentiments towards it. Say for example a company has declared high dividend. Now it is up to the investor to either invest in the stock or walk away from it. This will be based on the sentiment of the market. Here, you can choose to be a contrarian and go against the crowd or be a trend follower and buy the stocks. It might seem impossible in the beginning but will get easier as you go.

AI

Ai refers to artificial intelligence. Here, you will make use of software to predict the prices of the stocks. You will find this software easily. All you have to do is punch in the numbers and it will give you the results. But you have to understand that this software will not give you a 100% accurate result and only 80 to 90%. So, you will still have to do your research on the topic in order to find the best stocks to invest with.

These form the different prediction techniques that you can adopt.

Chapter 15: Basic Concepts of Forex Markets

There are some basic forex concepts that you have to acquaint yourself with if you wish to invest in it. Here are the concepts explained in detail.

Big 8

When it comes to the forex market, there are a few countries whose currency is quite strong. Strong currencies are a result of economic stability and how the countries manage their economy. These 8 major currencies are quite stable as well and will help you ring in a profit and you will not have to put in too much effort towards looking for the top currencies to invest in. The major 8 currencies include the US dollar, the Canadian dollar, the Euro, the UK pound sterling, the Swiss franc, the Australian dollar, the New Zealand dollar and the Japanese Yen. These are said to be the best currencies to invest with. They can be your strong currencies that you can pair with a few weak ones. However, you have to look up their rates from time to time as they change from time to time. You cannot expect the prices to remain at the same level for too long.

Buy in pairs

The forex market is quite unique. Unlike in a regular market where you pay your local money to buy stocks, you need not do the same in the forex market. So, when you have a certain currency in your possession, which is different from your home currency, you can exchange it for another currency. So, you will buy and sell simultaneously, within a single transaction. So, say you have 100 UD dollars with you. You wish to buy the yen. But in order to ring in a bigger profit, you will exchange the dollar for euro and then buy the yen. This will help you earn a bigger profit. So, it is important for you to look at the difference in prices of each currency and find the extremes. At first, you might find this a bit tricky, as you will first buy the foreign currency paying your local currency and then buy another one and then another. Finally, your aim will be to exchange that with another one and so on. This is an important aspect of forex and something you will have to learn in order to carry out trade.

Dual benefits

It is important to note here that holding on to foreign currency for an estimated period of time will prove to be dually beneficial to the investor. This means that the investor will be able to make money two ways, through a single investment. Now let us say he starts by investing 500 yen to buy euros. He will use the euros to buy himself a euro bond. He will then use the bond to earn a 10% interest for the next 2 years. But there is a catch here. The currency exchange rate should remain the same for this to happen. Now suppose the difference in currency rates remains the same, he will be able to capitalize on the latter. But if it changes, then he will have to lose some money, especially if yen increases in value. So, once he sells the bond, he will get the money back and add to it the profit that he will make from the interest that he gets paid. So, the investor will be left with two different sums at the end of it, which will make his investments worthwhile.

Pink sheets

The forex trade does not take place like regular trade and there is a small difference in it. This means that the investor might not be able to find the forex listing on the regular stock market and will have to buy them over the counter. Better known as pink sheets, the investor will have to approach an agent, who will have access to foreign currencies. He or she will be able to procure the currency for the investor through his connections. Here, you will not have to pull out money from your pocket to buy the currency. Instead, you will be issued pink sheets carrying the value of the money that you wish to invest in the market. These pink sheets are easy to trade with. You can exchange them for the currency of your choice and then exchange the currency for a sum based on the prevailing exchange rate.

Returns

The rate of return on foreign currencies is extremely high. The difference in exchange rates is quite volatile and might leave you with a big profit. But you should also be prepared for a big loss as the rates can swing both ways. So it will be difficult to say in which way the prices might swing. Some might say it is a safe investment and you will probably always see profits but some others might stay away from it owing to having suffered only losses through it. So, it is important for a trader to be prepared for extremes if he or she wishes to invest in the forex market.

These form the different basic concepts that you have to know about in order to invest in the forex market.

Chapter 16: Benefits of Forex Trading

Some investors opine that forex is the best trading option. There are many reasons for this claim and some of them are highlighted in this chapter.

Liquid market

When it comes to financial securities, liquidity is extremely important. It is a necessity for your security to have a ready audience otherwise you will not be able to profit from it. The forex market is quite liquid and you will not have to go through a lot to dispose of your currencies. There will be someone or the other in the market ready to buy what you have on offer and you will find it rather easy to sell your securities.

Global reach

The forex market has a global reach. This means that you can make foreign investments and diversify your portfolio. Many people wish to have foreign investments in their portfolio and forex will give you a great opportunity to do so. All you have to do is buy a currency of a foreign country and have it in your possession. You can then exchange it (either half or full) for a third country's currency and be left with foreign currencies. However, remember that you have to continue with it in order for it to qualify as a foreign investor. Trying it out for a month and then stopping with it abruptly will not count as you having made foreign market investments.

Open 24 hours

You will have the chance to buy and sell your stocks all through the day in the forex market. You need not wait for a day to sell your currencies. You can buy or sell it anytime you feel like. Sometimes, people wish to trade in currencies of countries whose timings are different from theirs. For this, they need not stay up at night as they can give the buy or sell call during their waking hours and then have the transaction completed overnight. So, it is ideal for people looking to trade with foreign countries that have a time zone difference.

Always bull

The forex market is known as a perpetual bull market, making it an ideal choice for beginners. This means that the market will always be bull and you don't have to worry about the prices dropping too low. In due course of time, you will see that there is not a dull moment in the fore market and you are able to translate most of your investments into profits.

No agents

Many people dread agents. They feel as though these are middlemen and will simply add to the costs. They might also have the power to alter the course of the currency, which might affect its final price. This is mostly seen as an unfair practice and what makes many investors stay away. However, since there are no middlemen in foreign currency trade, you need not worry about these issues and can freely invest in it. These trades will prove to be quite lucrative especially for those that wish to invest in high volumes.

Transaction costs

Transaction costs are reduced when it comes to forex trade. You need not worry about extra costs getting added on to your expenditure. This is not possible with some of the other types of stock market investments such as equity stocks and bonds. There, you will not have the chance to avoid these costs, as the middlemen will be present by default. So, even beginners will find it easy to start with forex trading. There will not be too many costs to begin with and the returns will be quite generous.

Easy to profit

As was mentioned before, it is possible for you to profit from forex. Forex trading is a simple form of trading and will leave you with a big profit at the end. But you have to study the market carefully and find the right currency pairs. You can also work closely with your broker if you wish and come up with a good investment plan. It is ideal for you to find a good strategy, especially if you wish to avail long-term benefits from your investments.

No majority

It is not possible for a certain group of investors to control the forex market. This means that they will not have the chance to control the rates of these currencies as nobody can invest large volumes. These currencies are traded all over the world and that makes it a very big market for an individual to control. So, you don't have to worry about just a few people controlling the market while the rest finding it difficult to have a control over the price fluctuations.

No limit

The forex market does not discriminate. So, regardless of whether you are a beginner or an experienced hand, the forex market will welcome you with open hands. There is no limit on how much you can buy or sell. You can also buy and hold, or sell it depending on your plan. There are no set rules to abide by and you can do as you wish. This makes forex a great platform to increase your investment's worth.

Knowledge

It is quite easy for you to acquire knowledge on forex. There are many places from where you can get information about foreign currencies and invest in them. All you need is the latest rates and difference in exchange values and you can start dealing in them. You need not have any relevant experience in forex or stock market investments for that matter and can easily invest in foreign currency. If you are unsure about something, then you can always discuss it with your broker and then buy the currency.

Guarantees

As you know, there are a few guarantees in the forex market. This means that you are guaranteed to have profits even if the prices of the currencies fluctuate. At no point will they be too low for you to not profit from. You need not worry about something slipping below your buying price. You can still remain with a profit regardless of whether you bought it on the same day or the previous.

These form just some of the advantages of forex markets but are not limited to these. You will get acquainted with the others once you start investing in forex.

Chapter 17: A Look at Penny Stocks and Real Estate

Penny stocks as you know refer to those that are priced at $5 or under. Here is looking at some of its aspects in detail.

Small value

The first and foremost aspect of these stocks is that they are valued at $5 or less. This means that they are affordable and you can buy a lot of them with just a small investment. These are valued low mainly because of the small size of the company. They will belong to companies that have a small investment and not too many employees. They will also have a small number of assets and possibly very little liability. All of this will go towards making their per share value low.

Information

One thing to understand about these stocks is that not information is available about them. You will not readily find information about them and will have to put in some effort towards it. Reading the newspaper or the stock market journal will make for a good start. You should look up information and might have to rely on your agents. If even they don't have the information, then you might have to rely on forums or message boards. You should ask your questions there and wait for them to be answered by an expert.

Intraday trade

Penny stocks are generally traded intraday. This means that most people that trade in penny stocks buy and sell them on the same day thereby not holding on to it for a long time. You too can do the same, especially if you wish to see quick gains. However, it is important for you to remain a little patient, as it will take you some time to find the best stocks. You cannot get started with it today and expect to see gains tomorrow. Wait at least a month before trading intraday with it.

Pink sheets

Pink sheets refer to over the counter transactions. Here, you need not make use of money to trade in the stocks. You can make use of pink sheets, which will contain an equivalent value of the money. You can exchange these sheets to but the stocks. This is great for all those that don't want to pay money for stocks that they will dispose of within the same day. Since most of these sticks are bought in the morning and disposed of in the evening, you will not have to make an arrangement for the finances.

Risk

What many people don't realize is even though penny stocks cost quite less they are probably high-risk investments. This is mainly owing to the fact that these investments are volatile and the prices will move high and low within the same day. There are cases of some stocks going high enough to give the investor 100% profit within one day and also cases where people have lost 100% owing to falling prices. So, it is really tough to predict a stock and it is important for you to be prepared for anything. Generally, those that remain vigil will be able to pick the right stocks and remain alert.

Brokers

One important aspect of penny stocks is that not many brokers will be interested in buying it for you. This is mainly because of the high degree risk that is attached with penny stocks. They will warn you and might not show interest in buying the socks for you. So, it will be a better option for you to buy and sell the stocks yourself.

These form the different aspects of penny stocks that you should be aware of in order to invest in it and reap profits. But it is advisable for you to be a little cautious and ensure that you do your research on the topic before making the investments.

Chapter 18: Real Estate Investments

Real estate investments are also lucrative choices for you. These are also generally classified as portfolio investments. Real estate investments have the potential of increasing your money's worth.

Choosing property

The first aspect is to choose the right property. The property should be in the ideal location. Remember that the location of the property will play a big role in helping you increase your money's worth. You will have to look in an area that is known to help property values double or triple in years. The next aspect to consider is the price. If you look for properties in posh areas, then you will have to pay a little extra for them. So, you should be ready for it. Next, you should check out the amenities in the area. Then you can choose the right property.

Buying

The buying process can be a bit time consuming but you should be prepared to go through it. After all, at the end of it, you will be left with an amazing house for yourself. There will be a few documents and papers to sign that the owner of the property might bring to you. You must go through them carefully in order to ensure that you know what you are signing on. Once done, the keys will be handed to you.

Selling

It is possible for you to save on quite a bit of tax by buying and selling property in loop. There are some taxation rules that you can look into and make use of. And if you and your spouse file joint taxation then you can double the benefits. Most people looking to take advantage of this scheme buy and sell in loop. They will buy a house, live for 2 years and then sell. Buy again, live for 2 years and sell. Doing so helps in remaining with quite a lot of money.

Chapter 19: Fundamentals and Technical for Stocks

There is both fundamental and technical analysis that you have to conduct on stocks in order to find the best one. In this chapter, we will look at both in detail.

Fundamental analysis

The fundamental analysis trading refers to understanding the basic functioning of the company by going through its reports. Here is what you will be looking at.

Balance sheet

The very first thing to look at is the balance sheet of the company. As you know, the balance sheet contains information on what the company's finances look like. You can see the assets and the liabilities to check the company's financial status. If the assets are more than the liabilities, then it is a good company. If the liabilities are more than the assets, then it is not such a good company to invest with. If you think the company is doing well then you can pick to invest with them.

Income statement

The income statement of the company is what will tell you how the company is earning money. As you know, it is important for all companies to earn an income in order to operate smoothly. For this, you have to check the money that is flowing in. one way will be through operating income and the other will be non-operating income. Operating income refers to the money that has come in through sale of their products and services. On the other hand, non-operating income is what it has earned through the sale of its assets. These assets can be its belongings that it has sold to remain in business. You might have to further investigate as to why they had to sell it and whether they did so to pay off debt.

Cash flow statement

The next thing is to check the company's cash flow statement. Cash flow statement refers to looking at the money that is coming in and also the money that is going out. You should see how much the company generally earns and spends. What they spend on and whether they have a transparent system. Looking at the cash flow statement will help you assess whether or not a company is good to invest with.

Earnings

You will have to calculate the earnings per share of a company. This is important as there will be lots of shares floating in the market and you have to see how much the company is making through the shares. There is a simple calculation that you can do to find the earnings per share. Once you find it, you should see whether the company is profiting from it or they have undervalued their shares. Based on the result you can decide to either invest with them or steer clear.

Price to book

The next thing to check is the price to book value. As you know, not all shares are listed at their book value there will be some whose book value will be different from their listed value. You will have to find out if the stock is being undervalued in the market or overvalued. If it is undervalued, then you have to capitalize on the opportunity and invest in it. If it is overvalued, then it is best for you to not invest with it.

These form the different fundamental analysis that you have to conduct. As you can see, you are bothered about what is happening in the company internally. You wish to see whether everything is good, especially with the board members. If you feel like there is a lot of bickering internally and the board members are not getting along well enough then it is best to not pick such a company.

Technical analysis

The next analysis is known as the technical analysis. You will have to look at the graph and spot a pattern in it. Here is what you will be looking at.

Direction

The first aspect is to see the direction that it is taking. All stocks will follow a certain pattern and move in a particular direction. This direction might be upwards or downwards depending on the stock. As you know, if the stock has a bearish tendency then it will move downwards and if it has a bullish tendency then it will move upwards. Based on how the price is moving, you can decide on whether you wish to invest with it or not. It is quite simple to judge the direction. You already know how to assess whether it is a bullish pattern or a bearish one. Based on the same, you can check whether the price will move up or down.

Speed

The next thing to check is the speed of the stock. See whether it is moving up or down quickly or slowly. Some will move fast while others will move slowly. It is up to you to determine whether you want a fast moving stock or a slow moving one. The former will give you quick results whereas the latter will give you slow results. Based on the type and amount of investment that you wish to make, you can choose the stocks.

Distance

Distance refers to how far the stock will travel. Some stocks travel really high and attain all time high whereas some will fall really low and attain an all-time low. You have to determine whether your stock is going through any of these phases.

These form the technical analysis that you will have to do to understand whether you have a good stock or a bad one.

If you think these are too tough to calculate then you can make use of software. But you should know that they will not give you 100% accuracy and should be prepared to do your own research and calculations.

Chapter 20: Fundamentals and Technical for Forex

Fundamental analysis

The fundamental analysis for forex is calculated in a completely different way. Here are some of the things that you will have to consider to read a currency fundamentally.

Interest rates

The interest rates of a country have a direct bearing on the currency of the country. A currencies value will increase if the interest rates are high and decrease if they are low. You have to know that these rates are never the same and keep rising and falling. You have to check the rate of interest that the country in general charges for borrowings and what it gives for deposits. That will give you an idea of how weak or strong the currency is.

Employment scene

The employment scene also has an impact on the currency. Depending on how many people are employed, the value of the currency will be high or low. If too many are employed, then its value will be high. There will be more buying power and the demand for money will be high. If there are too many unemployed then the value will be low as there will be a lot of money floating in the market. So, you have to study the employment scene to find a strong currency.

Prices

The commodity prices in the country also play a part in the value of the currency. High prices will mean that the currency is strong and low prices will have meant that the currency is weak. You should read the news regularly to see what's happening around the world and whether price differences in commodities are occurring. Based on it you can surmise whether the currency is weak or strong.

Gross domestic product

The GDP or gross domestic product of a country also has a bearing on the value of the currency. If the GDP is high, then it means the currency is strong. If the GDP is low, then it means that the currency is weak. You can know it based on annual reports that you can study.

Political scenario

The political scenario of a country also has a bearing on the value of the currency. Politicians determine many aspects of the country such as the interest rates and the other statistics that govern the central bank. Being aware of the political scenario of the country whose currency you wish to invest with will help you assess whether it is a strong currency or a weak one.

Natural calamities

Certain natural calamities also have a bearing on the price of a currency. Whether it is an earthquake or a tsunami, there will be considerable impact on the overall value of the currency. You will have to keep an eye on the news and withdraw from a currency if you think it will be negatively impacted or not invest in it until such time as it stabilizes.

Technical analysis

Now let us look at the technical analysis that you have to conduct on foreign currencies.

Moving averages

Moving averages are the most popular statistical analysis that people prefer to conduct on forex trades. The person looks at the pattern of the prices and determines where it is headed next. There are three types of moving averages namely simple, weighted and exponential. You can choose the one you think best.

Bollinger bands

Bollinger bands are the second most popular statistical technique that is employed. Here too, you will make use of statistical methods to find a pattern that the currency will follow.

RSI

RSI refers to relative strength index. Relative strength index is one that will help you assess whether a stock is priced right. As you know, some might be over priced and some underpriced. You have to look for the latter to invest with. Once you find the value you should see if it is lesser than 30 or greater than 70. If it is the former, then it is undervalued and if it is the latter then it is overvalued. You can make your choice based on the statistic.

Stochastic oscillator

The oscillator method is where you make use of a graph that moves back and forth within a set range, much like a pendulum. You will have to make use of statistical techniques to find the range. You can instead make use of software for the same.

Fibonacci series

As we had read earlier in the prediction techniques, it is possible for you to predict the trend of the stocks using Fibonacci numbers. Similarly, you can also predict forex prices using the same. The Fibonacci series is quite easy to understand. Once you do, you can implement it to find a certain pattern that the currency will follow.

Sentimental analysis

Sentimental analysis refers to understanding the mood or the sentiment of the investors and then investing in them. For this, you have to study the market and understand what a majority of them are going to do. Based on a piece of information or a news article, some might decide to buy or sell a particular currency and you can decide to either be a contrarian or a trend follower.

Key highlights

The stock market is a vast place where many types of transactions take place on a daily basis. The stock markets are where buyers and sellers of financial securities converge and engage in trade. It is fairly simple to understand how the market operates. It is governed by the theory of demand and supply. When something is in demand, its value rises. If it is not in demand, then its value falls. When its value rises, many people dispose of their stock to profit from it. This causes a lot of them to float in the market and brings down its value considerably and so on and so forth. So, it is quite simple for a person to start with stock market investments and they don't have to spend too much time understanding it.

However, it is important to get started with it on the right foot. You cannot start investing in it just by knowing how it works. You have to spend some time and prepare for it. The first thing is to start with a computer. You will need one to carry out trade. Next comes the trading account followed by a broker. Once done, you have to pick the best securities to invest with and then buy and sell them to remain with a profit. You can also maintain a record of your journey to see the progress. Remember that the stock market will not always leave you with a profit alone and you should also be ready to undertake risks.

There are many types of financial securities that you can buy in the stock market and is not limited to just equity stocks alone. Right from stocks to precious metals and forex, you can buy and sell any security that you like. But before you do so, you have to understand the meaning and also the pros and cons of each. It is hard to pick a winner amongst them, as all will have their fair share of advantages and disadvantages. Some might find it easy to start with stocks while others will find forex convenient. So, you have to pick the one that suits you the best and go with it.

When you invest in the stock market, there are certain rules to swear by. These refer to those that will help you make the right choices. For example, it is important for you to do your research and also invest with risk capital. Similarly, you have to sketch out a plan for yourself and not be greedy when it comes to profits. All of these will go a long way in helping you remain in profit. However, they will not guarantee not having losses, but you will at least be able to cut down on them as much as possible.

It is important for you to calculate the fundamentals and technical of stocks in order to make the most of your investments. These can be calculated making use of statistical tools or just by going through reports of the company. There are varying levels of analysis and you have to pick the one based on your convenience. However, it is best for you to perform all the analysis, as that will put you in a better position to judge whether the stock is a good one to pick.

When it comes to forex transactions the rules for fundamental and technical analysis changes considerably! We saw the different calculations that you must make with it and how it differs from what you might have to make with stocks. It is best for you to go through it again so that you know how exactly you can calculate the different statistics and use to your advantage. Some people might assume that all of this is unnecessary and it is best for them to simply go with their gut instinct. But, once you make use of these, you will see how useful it really is and how it will help you remain with a bigger profit at the end.

We looked at the different aspects of the forex market and also the advantages of investing in it. As you can see, it is a great platform for you to use and ring in profits. Of course you will have to do your due research on the subject and invest in it wisely. You need have too much knowledge on the subject and can easily buy and sell foreign currencies. If in case, you do have doubts then you can clarify with your broker and make all the right investments.

Penny stocks are great investment choices for those looking to invest a small sum but reap a big profit. Penny stocks are those that are priced at $5 or less. These stocks belong to small companies and the demand for these is quite high. So they will be traded in high volumes and will prove to be quite liquid. However, they can be a bit volatile and it is important for you to be a bit careful. You should do your research first and only then make an investment. Going into it without much research is a big no-no for any financial investment.

There are many prediction methods that you can choose from to predict stock price trends. Some of them include using candlesticks, Fibonacci numbers etc. We looked at them in detail and you can choose the one that you think is comfortable. However, since many types of software are easily available, you won't have to do too much manually. You can simply punch in the numbers and the computer will do the rest. You can then come to a conclusion and make the right move in the market.

If you wish to invest in the ideal company, there are some aspects that you have to consider first. This includes the reputation of the company, its age, the types of shareholders etc. Once you have understood all of this, you can decide on whether it is a good company to invest with. It is obvious that you will have to implement a unique strategy and not blindly copy someone else's. You will only be rewarded if you know what you want and go for it. Even if the company is looking bad on paper but you think it has the potential then you can take the risk of investing in it. But if you wish to play safe then you should avoid investing in it.

The same extends to stocks. You have to pick the right stocks based on some criteria. We looked at them in detail and you can go through them again if you wish to understand it in a better way.

As a last piece of advice, it is important for you to be patient in the stock market. You will be able to ring in profits no doubt, but you have to make the right moves at the right time and wait for something to grow in value over a period of time.

Conclusion

I thank you once again for choosing this book and hope you found it informative.

The main aim of this book was to educate you on the topic of stock market investments. I hope you have understood the different aspects of the market and are prepared to invest your money. I wish you luck with your stock market endeavors.

All the best!

Thank you for Reading! I Need Your Help...

Dear Reader,

I hope you Enjoyed "**Investing: Stocks, Options, Gold & Silver, Your Path To Wealth In A Bull Or Bear Stock Market**". I have to tell you, as an Author, I love feedback! I am always seeking ways to improve my current books and make the next ones better. It's readers like you who have the biggest impact on a book's success and development! So, tell me what you liked, what you loved, and even what you hated. I would love to hear from you, and I would like to ask you a favor, if you are so inclined, would you please share a minute to review my book. Loved it, Hated it - I'd just enjoy your feedback.

As you May have gleaned from my books, reviews can be tough to come by these days and

You the reader have the power make or break the success of a book. If you'd be so kind to review the book

https://www.amazon.com/review/create-review?ie=UTF8&asin=B015T8GCSG to review the book, I would greatly appreciate it!

Thank you so much again for reading "**Investing: Stocks, Options, Gold & Silver, Your Path To Wealth In A Bull Or Bear Stock Market**" and for spending time with me! I will see you in the next one!

Check Out More From The Publisher...

Construction: Purchasing Success Guide, Stay on Budget through your Supply Chain Management
by David Pollock
http://www.amazon.com/Construction-Purchasing-Management-Procurement-Estimating-ebook/dp/B010II2L1Y

Sales: Master the Art of Selling, Networking, and Time Management
by Grant Kennedy
http://www.amazon.com/Sales-Networking-Management-Productivity-Influence-ebook/dp/B0168V4N0W

Social Media: Master Social Media Marketing - Facebook, Twitter, YouTube & Instagram
by Grant Kennedy
http://www.amazon.com/Social-Media-Marketing-Facebook-Instagram-ebook/dp/B018Y68SWS

Gardening: Hydroponics for Beginners: The Ultimate Guide to Hydroponic Gardening
by Melissa Honeydew
http://www.amazon.com/Hydroponics-Sufficiency-Vegetables-Homesteading-Preservation-ebook/dp/B01508IZAS

Psychology: Hypnosis & Mind Control – To Overcome Stress, Anxiety, Depression & Finally Recover Your Happiness
by Fred McGaughy
http://www.amazon.com/Psychology-Hypnosis-Depression-Happiness-Brainwashing-ebook/dp/B014AMVA3E

www.ingramcontent.com/pod-product-compliance
Lightning Source LLC
Chambersburg PA
CBHW060405190526
45169CB00002B/760